CW01163457

from classroom to stardom

A Kids Guide to Becoming an Actor

sarah michaels

Copyright © 2023 by Sarah Michaels

All rights reserved.

No part of this book may be reproduced in any form or by any electronic or mechanical means, including information storage and retrieval systems, without written permission from the author, except for the use of brief quotations in a book review.

contents

Description	5
Introduction	7
1. DISCOVERING YOUR PASSION	15
Is Acting Your Calling? Let's Find Out!	15
Passion: Your Guiding Star on the Acting Journey	18
2. LEARNING ABOUT ACTING	21
The Acting Toolkit: Your First Steps on Stage and Screen	21
The School of Acting: Learning the Craft	23
3. STARTING SMALL	27
Small Beginnings: Your First Steps Onto the Stage	27
The Gifts of the Stage: Building Confidence and Skills	29
4. PRACTICING YOUR CRAFT	33
Practice Makes Perfect: The Golden Rule of Acting	33
The Actor's Toolbox: Method Acting and Other Techniques	35
5. FINDING YOUR UNIQUE VOICE	39
Finding Your Unique Spark: Developing Your Own Style and Voice in Acting	39
Uniquely You: The Power of Individuality in Acting	41

6. DEALING WITH REJECTION — 45
   Weathering the Storm: Facing Rejection and Setbacks in Acting — 45
   Bouncing Back: Tips on Dealing with Rejection and Setbacks — 48

7. THE AUDITION PROCESS — 51
   Ready, Set, Audition! What to Expect at an Audition — 51
   Shining Star! Tips for a Successful Audition — 53

8. GETTING AN AGENT — 57
   Agents of Change: How an Agent Can Propel Your Acting Career — 57
   The Agent Adventure: When and How to Consider Getting an Agent — 59

   Conclusion: Never Stop Dreaming — 63

description

Imagine embarking on a captivating journey into the enchanting world of acting, tailored just for young aspiring actors! This book is designed to ignite young minds' passion for storytelling and the performing arts, taking readers step-by-step through the thrilling, challenging, and rewarding path of becoming an actor.

Structured like a journey, the book introduces acting in all its fascinating forms—stage, film, voice-over, and more. Readers will dive into the nuts and bolts of acting, such as understanding scripts, expressing emotions, improvising, and even exploring various acting techniques. The emphasis on the importance of education, practice, and resilience forms the backbone of the narrative, encouraging readers to keep learning, practicing, and dreaming.

From starting with small roles and performances, understanding the role of an agent, to tackling auditions confidently, the journey is crafted to build readers' confidence and skills gradually. The book doesn't shy away from the tough aspects—like facing rejection and setbacks—but rather presents them as crucial stepping stones in the actor's journey, making it a genuine, relatable guide for young readers.

In a friendly and conversational tone, this book promises to be more than an informational read—it's a companion for every young reader dreaming of stepping into the spotlight. Designed to inspire, guide, and support, it encourages them to find their unique voice and style while fostering a love for the craft of acting. It's not just about how to become an actor—it's about inspiring readers to embrace their passion, dream big, and shine bright!

Sarah Michaels

introduction

what is acting? the wonderful world of performance

Hello there, young stars! Welcome to your very first step into the exciting, lively, and dynamic world of acting. Let's imagine acting as a grand, colorful, and sprawling landscape, filled with all sorts of exciting possibilities. It's a world that calls to those with stories in their hearts, who yearn to share these stories with others. That's right! Acting, at its very core, is storytelling. And you know what the most exciting part is? Everyone, including you, has the potential to become a great storyteller.

In the broadest sense, acting is the art of taking on the role of a character and bringing them to life. It's like

Introduction

donning a magical mask, not to hide who you are, but to become someone else, someone from a different time or place, with their own thoughts, feelings, and experiences. Isn't that an amazing power? You can become a knight from the medieval times, a futuristic robot, a school-going wizard, or even an animated fish seeking his lost son!

Now, let's dive a little deeper. You see, the vast landscape of acting isn't just a singular terrain; it's filled with different regions, each unique in its own way. Some of the most well-known are stage acting, film acting, and voice-over acting.

Firstly, let's take a look at stage acting. If you've ever seen a school play or a grand performance in a theatre, that's stage acting! Stage actors perform live in front of an audience. The energy here is electric, and the connection between the actors and the audience is direct and palpable. There's no 'take two' in stage acting, and that's where its thrill lies. Improvisation and quick-thinking come in handy when you forget a line or if something unexpected happens.

Secondly, there's film acting. When you watch movies or TV shows, you are witnessing film acting. This kind of acting reaches audiences through screens big and small all around the world. Unlike stage acting, film acting allows for multiple takes until the scene is just right. However, it requires a different set of skills as even the smallest of facial expressions can be captured and magnified on screen. The subtlety and nuance in your performance can truly make a difference here.

Then we have voice-over acting. Ever watched a cartoon or listened to an audio book? That's where voice-over actors shine! These actors lend their voices to characters, and it's their job to bring them to life using only their vocal talents. It might seem simple, but it requires a great deal of skill to convey a range of emotions and personalities through voice alone.

But the magic doesn't stop here. There's a variety of other acting forms as well, like musical theatre where you act, sing, and dance, or physical theatre that focuses on storytelling through movements more than words, or even puppetry where you control a puppet to tell a story!

While each of these forms of acting requires different techniques and skills, they all rely on the same foundation: the power of storytelling. Remember, the key is to convey the character's emotions and experiences so convincingly that the audience gets drawn into the story.

Are you ready to explore this vast landscape? To try on the magical mask of a character and step into their shoes? Remember, in the world of acting, the possibilities are as endless as your imagination! Acting isn't just about pretending to be someone else; it's about understanding them, connecting with them, and bringing them to life in your own unique way. It's a journey of discovery, not just of the characters you'll play, but also of yourself.

In this exciting world of acting, you are the storyteller, the adventurer, the explorer. And who knows? One day, you might even be the hero, the guiding light for others embarking on their own acting adventures. So, buckle up and get ready for a thrilling ride through the world of acting! You have many roles to play, stories to tell, and characters to bring to life. The stage is set, the camera is rolling, and the microphone is on. Let the magic begin!

every star begins with a spark

We've explored the magical world of acting and the many forms it can take, from the live thrill of the stage to the nuanced details of film, and the voice-driven artistry of cartoons and audiobooks. But now, you might be wondering, "Can I really be a part of this amazing world? Can I, too, become an actor?" The answer, my young friends, is an emphatic, "Yes!" Absolutely, positively, undeniably, yes!

Introduction

Do you know that every single actor you see, whether on a grand stage, in a blockbuster movie, or voicing your favorite animated character, once stood exactly where you are right now? They, too, were once curious about acting, just beginning to explore this colorful world. They, too, might have felt a mix of excitement, doubt, and a pinch (or maybe a handful) of nervousness. But they started somewhere, took that first brave step, and look where they are now!

Remember, everyone's journey into acting begins with a single step. That step might be joining a school drama club, participating in a local community play, or even putting on a puppet show for your family and friends in your backyard. No step is too small, no start is insignificant. Every effort you put into exploring acting, no matter how tiny it may seem, is a sparkling gem adding to your treasure trove of experience.

Now, you might be thinking, "But what if I don't get it right? What if I forget my lines or trip on the stage?" Let me let you in on a little secret: every actor, even the biggest stars, have made mistakes. They've forgotten lines, missed cues, or tripped over props. But do you know what they did next? They learned from it, they got up, dusted themselves off, and they carried on. Because in acting, just like in life, it's not about never falling down; it's about getting back up every time you do.

Introduction

Let's consider the journey of a seed. A tiny, unassuming seed has the potential to grow into a mighty tree. But it doesn't happen overnight. The seed needs to be nurtured, it needs sunlight, water, and care. Over time, with patience, the seed sprouts, grows, and eventually, stands tall as a strong tree. Just like the seed, your journey into acting will take time, patience, and nurturing. But rest assured, with dedication and hard work, your efforts will bear fruit.

You see, acting isn't about being perfect right from the start. It's about learning, growing, and constantly evolving. It's about exploring different characters, walking in their shoes, and sharing their stories. It's about expressing yourself and connecting with others. And every single person who has a story to tell, who is willing to learn and grow, can become an actor.

To embark on your acting journey, all you need is a dash of curiosity, a sprinkle of courage, and a generous helping of enthusiasm. It's about being brave enough to try, persistent enough to learn from your experiences, and passionate enough to keep going, even when the going gets tough. Remember, every stumble is an opportunity to learn, every challenge a chance to grow stronger.

My young friends, acting is a grand adventure awaiting you. It's a journey filled with creativity, excitement, and discovery. Just like every star in the sky begins as a tiny spark, every actor's journey begins with a small step. And who knows, you could be the next spark, ready to blaze a trail across the acting sky. So, embrace the thrill of the unknown, the joy of learning, and the magic of acting.

1 /
discovering your passion

is acting your calling? let's find out!

WE'VE BEEN on quite an adventure so far, haven't we? We've discovered what acting is, peeked into its many forms, and learned that every journey, no matter how grand, starts with a single step. But now comes an essential question: How do you know if acting is for you?

Just like a detective looks for clues, we're going to explore some signs that might show you're ready to leap into the world of acting. Don't worry; this won't be a search for fingerprints or a complicated code to decipher. Instead, it's more like a treasure hunt within yourself! Sounds exciting, right? Let's dive in!

First, let's consider storytelling. Do you find yourself captivated by stories? Perhaps you're the one at the campfire, weaving tales that have your friends hanging onto every word. Maybe you're the first to volunteer when your teacher asks for a story reader, or perhaps you're the one who adds imaginative twists to everyday events. If you find joy in narrating tales, creating characters, and sharing them with others, then that's your first clue. Remember, acting at its core is storytelling, and if you love telling stories, you're already one step ahead!

Now, think about impersonation. No, we're not talking about serious, professional impersonation here. It's more about the fun you might have had trying to walk like a penguin, or mimicking the way your cat yawns, or perhaps doing an impression of your favorite cartoon character. If you find excitement in exploring different behaviors, voices, or mannerisms, guess what? You're holding onto another clue! Actors often need to study and impersonate the characteristics of the characters they're playing. So, if you've got a knack for mimicry, you've got the acting bug in you!

Finally, let's reflect on performing. Have you ever felt a rush of excitement being in front of an audience? It could be anything from reciting a poem in your school assembly, presenting a project in front of your class, or even performing a funny dance at a family gathering. If you feel a connection with the audience, if their laughter, applause, or attentive silence makes your heart flutter with joy, then my friend, you've discovered another clue! Acting is all about performance, and the thrill of captivating an audience is a telltale sign of a budding actor.

You see, these clues are like little stars that guide you towards the world of acting. They're not about being the best; instead, they're about the excitement, joy, and fulfillment that storytelling, impersonation, and performing bring you. The most wonderful thing is, these signs are not boxes to check off a list, but stepping stones leading you to discover your passion.

The journey into acting is not just about talent; it's also about passion, dedication, and the sheer joy of becoming someone else, even if it's just for a moment. The world of acting welcomes all, not because they are perfect, but because they are passionate. And if you've seen these signs in you, then you're not just ready, but excited to dive into this magical world!

But what if you're still unsure? That's perfectly alright! Remember, every journey is unique. You might need to explore more, try different things, and listen to your heart. Acting is a vast world, filled with different paths. Whether you want to tell stories, impersonate characters, or perform in front of an audience, there's a place for you in this magical landscape. So, let your heart guide you, let your passion lead the way, and embark on this journey of self-discovery.

passion: your guiding star on the acting journey

We've uncovered some clues about your interest in acting, and now we're all set to delve deeper into a very crucial ingredient of your acting journey: passion. Think of passion as a guiding star, bright and ever-present, leading you on your path towards becoming an actor. It's an inner spark that illuminates your journey, turning hard work into a rewarding adventure. Sounds magical, right? Let's dive in to understand how this powerful force can shape your acting journey.

Have you ever observed a painter absorbed in their work, oblivious to the world, as they carefully dab colors onto a canvas, creating a masterpiece? Or perhaps you've noticed a dancer, lost in the rhythm of the music, their movements telling a beautiful story. This absorption, this dedication, is driven by passion. And just like the painter and the dancer, as an actor, your passion becomes the driving force behind your storytelling, your performances, and your journey to connect with the audience.

When you're passionate about something, it doesn't feel like work. It feels like an adventure, a journey you're excited to embark on. Practicing lines, understanding a character, or rehearsing scenes might seem like hard work. But when fueled by passion, these tasks transform into exciting challenges, puzzles waiting to be solved, and opportunities for growth and creativity. It's your passion that makes you want to dive deeper, reach higher, and push beyond the limits.

Passion also gives you the resilience to bounce back from setbacks. Remember, in the world of acting, not everything will always go according to plan. You might forget lines, your performance might not come out as expected, or you might face rejection. But it's your passion, your love for acting, that helps you stand up, dust off the disappointment, and say, "I'll try again." It's your unwavering desire to learn, grow, and improve that turns these bumps into stepping stones, propelling you towards your dream.

Let's not forget, your passion for acting shines through in your performances. It's the spark that makes your character's emotions feel real, their story engaging, and their world immersive. When you perform with passion, you're not just playing a character, but living their life, feeling their feelings, and sharing their story. This passion radiates from you, reaching the hearts of your audience, captivating them, and drawing them into the narrative.

However, passion is not a one-time thing; it's a flame that needs to be continuously kindled. You can fuel your passion by continually learning, exploring different characters, trying various forms of acting, and seeking inspiration from the world around you. Remember, every actor has a unique passion story. Your passion might stem from your love for storytelling, your interest in exploring different characters, or your joy in connecting with an audience. The key is to identify this driving force, embrace it, and let it guide you in your acting journey.

In this magical world of acting, passion is your guiding star, your compass, and your driving force. It's what turns hard work into a rewarding journey and challenges into opportunities. So, keep your passion alive, let it illuminate your path, and remember, it's your unique spark that will make you stand out in the dazzling sky of acting.

Are you ready to let your passion guide you? Are you excited to let it transform hard work into a thrilling adventure, setbacks into learning opportunities, and your performances into captivating narratives? Then hold on to your passion, let it fuel your acting journey, and get ready to immerse yourself in the magic of storytelling, the joy of performance, and the thrill of becoming a character. The world of acting awaits you, ready to be illuminated by your passion and your stories!

2 / learning about acting

the acting toolkit: your first steps on stage and screen

WE'VE EXPLORED passion and how it acts as your guiding star on the acting journey. Now, let's roll up our sleeves and get our hands on some practical tools you'll need in your acting toolkit. Think of these as your magical equipment that helps you bring characters to life. Intriguing, right? Let's get started!

First up, understanding scripts. Now, a script may seem like just a bunch of lines written on paper, but it's actually a treasure map. It gives you clues about your character, the story, and your role in it. Reading a script is like going on a quest to understand your character's world. Look beyond the lines your character speaks. Ask questions like, "Why does my character say this?"

or "What is my character feeling here?" This detective work will help you bring authenticity and depth to your performance.

Next in our toolkit is expressing emotions. Acting is all about sharing your character's feelings and experiences with your audience. But how do you laugh, cry, or show fear as your character? A handy tip is to draw from your own experiences. Remember how you felt when you lost your favorite toy, or when you won a game? Use those memories to help you portray your character's feelings. The more authentic your emotions are, the more your audience will connect with your character.

Thirdly, we have improvisation. Think of it as a magical power that helps you adapt and create in the moment. Sometimes, things might not go as planned during a performance. Maybe you forget a line, or a prop isn't where it's supposed to be. That's where improvisation comes in! It allows you to think on your feet and keep the story going. And who knows, you might even discover a new aspect of your character while improvising!

Lastly, but certainly not least, is listening and reacting. Yes, you heard that right! Acting isn't just about delivering lines; it's also about reacting to what other characters say or do. This helps your performance feel more real and dynamic. Imagine you're having a conversation with a friend. You don't just wait for your turn to speak, do you? You react to what they're saying, and that's exactly what you need to do in acting as well.

Let's not forget, all these tools are linked by one key factor: practice. The more you use these tools, the more skilled you'll become at using them. It's like learning to play a new instrument. At first, you might hit a few wrong notes, but with practice, you'll be playing beautiful melodies.

Acting is an exciting journey of exploring characters, sharing stories, and connecting with audiences. And these tools in your acting toolkit are your faithful companions on this journey. They're here to help you delve into your character's world, share their emotions, adapt to surprises, and react to the world around them.

the school of acting: learning the craft

By now, we've journeyed through the magical world of acting, discovered the tools of the trade, and learned how passion can illuminate your path. Now, let's turn the spotlight onto something equally exciting and very important: learning the craft of acting through education. Ready to open the doors to this fascinating classroom? Let's step in together!

Education in acting is like a treasure chest filled

with jewels of knowledge. It gives you an understanding of the craft, equips you with techniques, and offers guidance under expert mentors. Think of attending acting classes or workshops as embarking on an exciting quest to gain these precious jewels.

Acting classes are like a laboratory where you can experiment with your skills in a safe environment. Here, you can explore a range of emotions, try out different characters, and even make mistakes without any fear. The best part? Every misstep is a chance to learn and grow. It's like a rehearsal before the grand performance!

In acting workshops, you get to learn from experienced actors and instructors who have trodden the path you're now stepping onto. They can offer valuable insights, share their experiences, and guide you through your acting journey. You can learn how they tackled challenges, how they prepared for their roles, and even some secret tips and tricks of the trade!

Another great thing about acting classes is the chance to meet fellow aspiring actors. These are your comrades in the magical world of acting. You can learn from each other, share your experiences, and even practice together. Remember, acting is not a solitary adventure; it's a journey shared with other storytellers, and these friendships can add a lot of joy to your acting adventure.

Moreover, attending acting classes or workshops can help you understand different styles and forms of acting. You may be introduced to theatre acting, film acting, voice-over acting, and more. Each of these has unique techniques and approaches, and learning about them can help you decide which path you want to explore further.

But let's pause for a moment here. It's important to remember that attending acting classes or workshops doesn't mean you'll become a perfect actor overnight. Just like a seed needs time to grow into a tree, your acting skills need time to develop. You might start with small roles, make mistakes, and face challenges. But every step you take in the learning journey is a step closer to becoming the actor you aspire to be.

Now, let's get one thing clear: attending acting classes or workshops doesn't make you any less talented or passionate. Instead, it's a sign of your commitment to learning and improving, your dedication to your craft, and your eagerness to become the best actor you can be. It shows that you're not just dreaming about becoming an actor; you're working towards it!

Education in acting is an exciting journey of learning, experimenting, and growing. Whether it's attending acting classes or workshops, every moment spent learning is a precious jewel added to your acting treasure chest.

So, future stars, are you ready to step into the school of acting, to learn, experiment, and grow? Are you excited to gather these precious jewels of knowledge and equip yourselves for the magical journey of acting? Get set to turn the spotlight onto learning, because in the grand theatre of acting, every lesson learned is a step towards a standing ovation! Let's embark on this exciting quest of learning and let the magic of acting unfold!

3 / starting small

small beginnings: your first steps onto the stage

WE'VE JOURNEYED through the worlds of passion, acting basics, and education in acting. Now, let's shine the spotlight on your first steps onto the stage. Every great actor begins somewhere, often in small roles and performances. And guess what? That's exactly where we're headed. Are you ready to explore this exciting part of the journey? Let's dive in!

Think of your first roles as the seedlings of your acting career. They might seem small and insignificant, but with time, care, and effort, they can grow into a forest of amazing performances. And where can you find these seedlings? Well, you don't have to look far!

Opportunities are all around you, in school plays, community theater, or even in creating your own performances.

Let's start with school plays. Participating in a school play can be an exciting adventure. Whether you're playing the lead or a supporting role, each character is important and offers unique opportunities to learn and grow. Plus, school plays give you a chance to experience the thrill of performing in front of a live audience. Remember, every line you speak, every emotion you express, and every applause you receive is a step forward in your acting journey.

Next up is community theater. This is like a bigger stage where you can interact with a diverse group of actors and audience. It offers a chance to work with directors, learn from more experienced actors, and immerse yourself in different stories. Don't shy away from small roles. They're like hidden gems, packed with potential for you to showcase your acting skills.

And let's not forget, you can also create your own performances. Yes, you heard it right! This is where your creativity can truly shine. You can write your own script, create characters, and even direct your own play. It's like being a magician, creating a whole new world from your imagination. And the best part? It offers an opportunity to learn about different aspects of a performance, not just acting.

Now, you might be wondering, "But I want to play bigger roles. I want to be the star of the show!" And that's a great aspiration. Remember, though, even the biggest stars started with small roles. What matters is not the size of the role, but how you play it. It's your opportunity to showcase your talent, your creativity, and your passion for acting. It's your chance to learn, grow, and evolve as an actor.

Consider every role, big or small, as an opportunity to explore different characters, express various emotions, and connect with your audience. Treat each performance as a learning experience, a chance to improve, and a step forward in your acting journey.

the gifts of the stage: building confidence and skills

Let's now shine a light on a hidden treasure of acting that we haven't explored yet: the value of acting experiences in building confidence and skills. We've talked about starting with small roles and performances, but what exactly do these experiences give you, besides a fun time and a round of applause? Well, they're secretly helping you grow as a person and as an actor. Intrigued? Let's unveil the magic together!

First and foremost, acting is an incredible confidence booster. Imagine standing on a stage, with all eyes on you, as you transform into another character. It's a brave act, isn't it? Every time you step on stage, you're not just stepping into a character's shoes, you're stepping into a space of courage. With each performance, you'll notice that you're becoming more self-assured, not only on stage but also in your daily life.

Take a moment to remember your first performance. You were probably a bundle of nerves, right? But guess what? You did it! You faced the audience and played your part, despite the butterflies in your stomach. That's a huge win! And every time you perform, you'll find that those butterflies become less daunting and more like friendly companions. That's your confidence growing!

Now, let's talk about skills. Every role you play, every script you read, and every emotion you express is a unique lesson in acting. You're building a repertoire of characters and emotions that you can tap into for future performances. With each role, you're learning to adapt to different characters, express a range of emotions, and improvise when needed.

And it's not just acting skills you're building. Remember the time when you had to memorize your lines for a play? You were sharpening your memory skills. Or that time when you had to coordinate a scene with your fellow actors? You were developing your teamwork skills. And when you created your own performance, you were harnessing your creativity and leadership. Isn't it wonderful how acting secretly helps you grow in so many ways?

Moreover, these experiences also help you understand your strengths and areas you can improve. Maybe you're great at comedy, or you have a knack for dramatic roles. Maybe you need to work on your stage presence or voice modulation. Either way, every experience is an opportunity to learn more about yourself as an actor.

But here's the most wonderful thing. With each performance, each applause, each lesson learned, you're becoming a storyteller. You're learning to connect with the audience, to share your character's story, to make people laugh, cry, or think. And this, my young thespians, is the heart of acting: storytelling.

Acting is an adventure, a journey of self-discovery, learning, and growth. Every role, every performance, is a step towards becoming a confident individual and a skilled actor. They're not just roles; they're opportunities to express, connect, learn, and shine.

So, aspiring actors, are you ready to embark on this journey of building confidence and skills? Are you excited to see where these stepping stones lead you? Remember, the stage is a magical place that transforms you into characters, but also helps you grow as an individual. Let's step onto the stage, embrace the lessons it offers, and let the magic of acting unfold. The spotlight is on, the curtains are drawn, and the stage is all yours. Let's make some magic happen!

4 /
practicing your craft

practice makes perfect: the golden rule of acting

WE'VE JOURNEYED through the magical world of acting, taken our first steps onto the stage, and discovered the hidden treasures of confidence and skills. Now, let's set our sights on an important milestone on this acting journey: practice. Yes, you've probably heard the phrase "practice makes perfect" before, but do you know how crucial it is in the realm of acting? Buckle up, because we're about to dive into this fascinating adventure!

Imagine acting as a giant canvas and you're the artist. Each line you speak, each emotion you express, and each character you play are the colors you use to paint your masterpiece. And how do you create a beautiful painting? By practicing your strokes. That's precisely what rehearsing lines, practicing emotions, and participating in acting exercises are: the practice strokes in your acting masterpiece.

Let's talk about rehearsing lines first. These are the words that bring your character to life. They are like the map that guides you through your character's journey. Rehearsing them helps you understand your character better and express their emotions effectively. But remember, it's not just about memorizing the lines; it's about understanding them, feeling them, and delivering them in a way that tells your character's story.

Now, what about practicing emotions? Well, let's face it; acting is all about expressing emotions. Whether it's happiness, sadness, anger, or excitement, your job as an actor is to make your audience feel what your character is feeling. Practicing emotions in front of a mirror can be a fantastic way to learn how to express different emotions convincingly. Watch your face as you transition from one emotion to another. This is your chance to explore the vast landscape of emotions and become a master of expression!

And then come the acting exercises. These are like the training ground for your acting skills. They can help you improve your voice projection, body language, improvisation skills, and much more. These exercises are like workouts for your acting muscles, strengthening them and preparing them for the grand performance.

But why is practice so crucial? Well, think of it as the bridge between learning about acting and actually performing. It's one thing to learn about expressing emotions or delivering lines, but quite another to do it in a performance. Practice helps you build this bridge, allowing you to transform your knowledge into action.

Practicing also helps you build confidence. With each line you rehearse, each emotion you practice, and each exercise you do, you're becoming more comfortable and confident as an actor. It's like a rehearsal before the grand show, preparing you for the spotlight.

So, aspiring actors, it's time to embrace the power of practice! Whether it's rehearsing your lines, practicing emotions in front of a mirror, or participating in acting exercises, each moment of practice is a precious gem that adds to your acting treasure. It's your chance to hone your skills, to grow as an actor, and to prepare yourself for the spotlight.

the actor's toolbox: method acting and other techniques

We've talked about practice, the golden rule of acting, and now it's time to add some more tools to your acting toolkit. Yes, acting is like building a fascinating character from a script, and to do that effectively, you need a set of techniques. Among these, a famous one is called 'Method Acting.' But don't worry, we'll talk about some others as well. Ready to expand your acting horizons? Let's start!

'Method Acting.' It sounds fancy, right? But it's a really cool concept! This technique asks actors to dive deep into their characters, so much so that they 'become' them, even off-stage. It means really understanding your character's emotions and motivations, using your own feelings and experiences to make the character feel real.

Let's imagine you're playing a character who loves ice cream. As a Method actor, you would spend time eating and enjoying ice cream yourself, thinking about what it feels like, the joy it brings, and then using those experiences when you play the character. This way, your performance becomes more genuine and believable.

But remember, Method Acting isn't about forgetting who you are. It's about using your own emotions as a guide to explore your character's feelings. It's a journey deep into the heart of the character you're portraying, a journey that brings them to life in a truly magical way.

Now, let's talk about a different technique called 'Classical Acting.' This technique is all about using your voice, body language, and facial expressions to express your character's emotions. It places a lot of importance on understanding the text, the play or the script, and rehearsing until you can deliver your lines and express your character's emotions flawlessly.

Then there's 'Meisner Technique,' named after its creator, Sanford Meisner. This technique focuses on 'living truthfully under imaginary circumstances.' Sounds fun, right? It encourages actors to respond instinctively to the situations and other characters in the play. It's all about being in the moment, just like in real life!

And there are many more techniques like these. Each one offers a unique way to approach acting, giving you more tools to bring your characters to life. As you learn more about acting, you'll find the techniques that work best for you, shaping your unique style as an actor.

Why are these techniques important, you may ask? Well, they're like secret codes that help you unlock your character's true essence. They guide you on how to walk in your character's shoes, how to talk like them, how to feel like them. They help you transform from being yourself to being 'in character.'

So, budding actors, are you excited to try these techniques? It might feel a bit tricky at first, but remember, every great actor was once a beginner. With practice and dedication, you'll master these techniques and create performances that are truly captivating.

As we explore these acting techniques, remember, they're not rules set in stone. They're guides, suggestions, tools to help you on your acting journey. Feel free to experiment with them, mix and match them, and create your own unique approach to acting. After all, acting is all about creativity and expression, and there's no one way to do it.

The world of acting is like a vast ocean of possibilities, and these techniques are your compass, guiding you as you navigate through your unique acting journey. So, let's grab our compass, set sail, and let the winds of creativity take us on an unforgettable adventure in the magical world of acting. Ready to explore? Let's go!

5 /
finding your unique voice

finding your unique spark: developing your own style and voice in acting

WE'VE BEEN on quite a journey together, haven't we? We've learned about the many dimensions of acting, from understanding characters to practicing lines, to exploring different acting techniques. Now, let's turn the spotlight towards you, specifically, to find your unique style and voice in acting. Yes, you heard it right! Acting is not just about mimicking others; it's about discovering and expressing your own unique flair. Ready to embark on this exciting journey of self-discovery? Let's dive in!

Let's start by understanding what 'style' and 'voice' mean in the world of acting. Your 'style' is your unique approach to acting, the way you express emotions, deliver lines, and bring characters to life. It's like your signature as an actor. Your 'voice,' on the other hand, isn't just about how you sound. It's about the messages you want to share and the impact you want to make through your performances.

But how do you discover your unique style and voice? Well, it's a journey of exploration, reflection, and experimentation. And the best part? You're already on this journey! Every character you play, every emotion you express, and every line you deliver is a step towards finding your unique style and voice.

One of the best ways to start is by exploring a range of characters and genres. From a brave hero to a cunning villain, from comedy to drama, each one will challenge you in different ways and help you discover your strengths and preferences.

But remember, it's not about copying others. It's okay to look up to your favorite actors, learn from them, and be inspired by their performances. But your goal is not to become a copy of them. Instead, you're aiming to use what you've learned to shape your own unique approach to acting.

You can think of it like baking a cake. You start with the same basic ingredients that all bakers use, but it's how you mix them together, how you add your own special touch that makes your cake unique. Similarly, you can learn the same techniques and play the same characters as other actors, but it's your unique interpretation and expression that will make your performance unique.

Developing your unique style and voice also means being true to yourself. It's about expressing your own feelings, thoughts, and experiences through your characters. It's about letting your own personality shine through your performances.

And finally, it's about being brave enough to experiment, make mistakes, and learn from them. Remember, acting is a journey of growth and learning, and every mistake is an opportunity to learn and improve. So, don't be afraid to try different things, to take risks, and to step out of your comfort zone.

Now, let's step into the limelight of self-expression! As we develop our unique style and voice, let's remember to stay true to ourselves, to express our own feelings and thoughts, and to use our performances as a canvas to paint our unique colors. After all, in the grand theatre of acting, it's our uniqueness that makes us shine.

uniquely you: the power of individuality in acting

We've been on an amazing journey together, haven't we? We've explored the vast world of acting, delved deep into character emotions, and even started to uncover our own unique style and voice. Now, we're going to discuss something incredibly important - the power of individuality in acting. You're each special in your own way, and it's this uniqueness that will make you truly shine on stage and screen. Ready to discover the power of being uniquely you? Let's get started!

Think about your favorite actors for a moment. What makes them stand out? It's not just their acting skills, right? It's also their individuality - the unique way they bring characters to life, the unique voice they add to their performances. This uniqueness is a testament to the power of individuality in acting.

So, what do we mean when we talk about individuality? It's about being true to yourself and bringing your unique perspective and personality into your performances. It's about showcasing who you are through your acting.

Individuality is like your superpower in acting. It's what sets you apart from other actors. It's what makes your performances memorable and special. It's what makes you, you!

How can you bring individuality into your acting, you ask? Well, it starts with understanding and accepting yourself. It's about acknowledging your strengths and weaknesses, your likes and dislikes, your dreams and fears. It's about knowing who you are and being proud of it.

Once you know yourself, you can bring this knowledge into your acting. Let's say you're naturally funny and love making people laugh. You can bring this into your performances, adding a touch of humor even to serious scenes, creating moments that are uniquely yours.

Bringing your individuality into your acting also means interpreting characters and scripts in your unique way. You might read a script and imagine the character in a way no one else does. That's your individuality shining through. It's your unique interpretation that will make your performance stand out.

Now, this doesn't mean you should ignore the director's instructions or disregard the script. It's about adding your unique touch within the framework of the character and the story. It's about collaborating with the director and the rest of the cast to create a performance that's true to the script and true to you.

Individuality in acting also means being brave. It's about daring to be different, daring to break stereotypes, daring to challenge the status quo. It's about making choices that may not be popular, but feel right to you. It's about standing up for your artistic vision, even when others might not understand it.

But remember, individuality is not about being

selfish or disregarding others. It's about expressing yourself while respecting the story, the character, the director, and your fellow actors. It's about contributing to the collective magic of the performance with your unique magic.

As we journey into the heart of individuality, let's remember that it's our uniqueness that makes us special. Let's celebrate our individuality and let it shine through in our performances. After all, in the grand theatre of acting, it's not about being better than others; it's about being the best version of ourselves.

6 /
dealing with rejection

weathering the storm: facing rejection and setbacks in acting

ON OUR JOURNEY through the world of acting, we've explored the fun parts like learning to express emotions, finding your unique voice, and showcasing your individuality. But now it's time to discuss something a bit more serious, but just as important - the inevitability of facing rejection and setbacks in an acting career. I know, it doesn't sound like much fun, but stick with me. Learning to navigate these tough times is a big part of becoming a great actor. Ready to learn more? Let's dive in!

First, let's talk about rejection. It's never fun, right? Whether it's not getting picked for the soccer team or not being invited to a birthday party, it can hurt. In the world of acting, rejection can come in the form of not getting a role you really wanted. You might have practiced for weeks, nailed the audition (or so you thought), and then...nothing. You don't get the part. It's tough. It's disappointing. But guess what? It's also normal.

Even the biggest actors you can think of have faced rejection. Do you know that Hollywood superstar Harrison Ford was told he would never make it in the movie business? Or that Meryl Streep was once deemed "ugly" for a movie role? But look at them now! They didn't let rejection stop them, and neither should you.

Rejection isn't a measure of your talent or your worth. It's just a part of the process. Sometimes, it's not even about you. It could be that the director had a different vision for the character or that someone else just fit the role a little better.

So, how do we handle rejection? It's all about perspective. Instead of seeing it as a failure, see it as a learning opportunity. Ask for feedback, find out what you could do better next time. And remember, each 'no' is one step closer to a 'yes.'

Now, let's talk about setbacks. A setback is when something slows down your progress or throws you off your path. In acting, a setback could be an illness that stops you from performing, a show that gets cancelled, or a scene that you just can't get right no matter how hard you try. Setbacks can be frustrating, but just like rejection, they're a normal part of life and acting.

When you face a setback, the most important thing is not to give up. It's okay to feel upset or frustrated, but don't let those feelings stop you. Instead, use them as fuel to work harder and come back stronger. Remember, setbacks are just temporary. They can slow you down, but they can't stop you unless you let them.

Facing rejection and setbacks can be tough, but they're also a chance to grow. They teach us resilience, the ability to bounce back from tough times. They teach us perseverance, the will to keep going no matter what. And they teach us humility, the ability to accept our weaknesses and learn from our mistakes. These are valuable life skills, not just for acting, but for everything you do.

So, let's not fear rejection or setbacks. Instead, let's see them as steps on our journey to becoming great actors. Let's learn from them, grow from them, and come back stronger.

bouncing back: tips on dealing with rejection and setbacks

We're at an important stop on our acting journey. In the last chapter, we talked about some of the tougher parts of acting: dealing with rejection and setbacks. But remember, while these experiences can be challenging, they can also help you grow into a stronger, better actor. Now, let's discuss some strategies and tips to handle these experiences and continue moving forward. Ready? Onward we go!

Firstly, let's talk about dealing with rejection. Remember, even the most successful actors faced rejection at some point in their career. So, when you experience it (and you will), don't take it personally. Here are a few tips to deal with rejection:

1. Stay Positive: It's easy to feel down after a rejection, but remember, it's not a reflection of your talent or worth. Stay positive, and remember, every no is just a step closer to a yes!

2. Learn from the Experience: Instead of letting rejection discourage you, use it as a learning opportunity. Ask for feedback. What could you have done better? Use this knowledge to improve your next audition.

3. Keep Practicing: Don't let a rejection stop you

from doing what you love. Keep practicing, keep improving, and keep auditioning.

Now, let's discuss how to handle setbacks. A setback could be anything that slows down your progress. But remember, a setback is just a delay, not a defeat. Here's how you can bounce back:

1. Acknowledge Your Feelings: It's okay to feel disappointed or frustrated when a setback happens. Acknowledge these feelings, but don't dwell on them.

2. Problem Solve: Identify what caused the setback and think of ways to overcome it. Did you forget your lines because of nerves? Maybe practicing relaxation techniques could help.

3. Get Back On Track: Don't let a setback keep you down. Once you've figured out a solution, get back on track. Keep practicing, keep performing, and keep chasing your dreams.

Having a strong support system can be a big help in dealing with rejection and setbacks. This could be your family, friends, or even your acting teacher or coach. Don't be afraid to talk about your feelings with them and ask for advice.

One more thing, always remember why you love acting. Remember the joy it brings you, the thrill of stepping into a new character, the magic of storytelling. When times get tough, this love for acting can be your guiding light, reminding you why all the hard work, the rejections, and the setbacks are worth it.

Dealing with rejection and setbacks can be tough, but remember, they're just part of the journey. They're not roadblocks, but stepping stones leading you to become a better, stronger actor. With a positive mindset, a willingness to learn, and a never-give-up attitude, you'll be ready to face any challenges that come your way.

7 /
the audition process

ready, set, audition! what to expect at an audition

NOW THAT WE'VE mastered dealing with rejection and setbacks, we're moving on to another exciting aspect of acting: auditions. You might have heard the word 'audition' before, but do you know what it really means? Well, let's unravel this mystery together and take a peek behind the curtain of an audition.

First things first, what is an audition? An audition is a performance you give in front of the people who are casting a play, a movie, or even a commercial. These people could be directors, producers, casting directors, and sometimes, even the writer. They're looking to see if you're the right fit for a specific role.

It's kind of like trying out for a sports team. You show them your skills, and if they like what they see, you might get picked!

Now, let's get into the nitty-gritty of what to expect during an audition.

1. Preparation: Before the audition, you'll usually receive a 'sides.' A sides is a small piece from the script that you'll be asked to perform. It might be a monologue or a dialogue. You'll need to learn your lines and understand your character. It's also a good idea to learn about the story and the other characters. This will help you give a more accurate performance.

2. Arrival: On the day of the audition, it's important to arrive early. This gives you time to relax and get comfortable with the surroundings. It's okay to feel a bit nervous, everybody does! Take a few deep breaths and remind yourself that you're prepared and ready.

3. The Performance: When it's your turn, you'll be called into the audition room. There might be several people in the room. Don't worry, they're there to see you shine! You'll introduce yourself and maybe have a little chat before you start. Then, you'll perform your sides. Remember, they're not just looking for people who can recite lines. They want to see if you can become the character.

4. Feedback and Direction: After you perform, the casting directors might give you some feedback. They

might ask you to try the scene again with a different emotion or a different approach. This doesn't mean you did something wrong. They just want to see if you can take direction and how versatile you can be.

5. The Wrap Up: Once you're done, you'll thank the casting directors for their time, and then you leave. They usually won't tell you if you got the part right away. That's normal. You'll hear from them later on, usually through a call or email.

Remember, each audition is a new experience and an opportunity to learn. Even if you don't get the part, be proud of yourself for trying. Each audition makes you a better actor.

As we close this chapter, remember that auditions are part of your acting adventure. It's where you get to show your skills, your understanding of the character, and your ability to take directions.

shining star! tips for a successful audition

Having just learnt about what auditions are and what they look like, let's turn our attention to how you can shine your brightest during these important moments. Here's a treasure chest of tips and advice to help you give an audition that you can be proud of!

1. Know Your Role: First up, get to know your char-

acter. Read your sides thoroughly and try to understand who you are portraying. Is your character happy or sad, loud or quiet, adventurous or timid? Understanding your character will help you deliver a more convincing performance.

2. Practice Makes Perfect: Practice your lines until you can say them in your sleep! The more comfortable you are with your lines, the more you can focus on how you're saying them, not just what you're saying. This brings your character to life.

3. Time Management: Make sure you manage your time well. Aim to arrive early for your audition. This gives you a chance to relax, observe your surroundings, and gather your thoughts before you step into the spotlight.

4. Dress the Part: Dress comfortably but also consider your character. You don't need a full costume, but if your character is a pirate, maybe wear a striped shirt. If your character is a ballerina, maybe wear something light and flowy.

5. Body Language: Remember, acting isn't just about the words you say; it's also about how you say them. Use your body language to express your character's feelings and thoughts. A surprised character might have wide eyes, a sad character might look down, and an angry character might have clenched fists.

6. Expressive Voice: Just like your body, your voice is a powerful tool. A soft voice can show sadness or fear, a loud voice can show anger or excitement, and changing your pace can build tension or show relief. Play with your voice and see what works for your character.

7. Take Direction: Be ready to take direction during your audition. The casting directors may ask you to try a scene in a new way. This doesn't mean you did something wrong. They're just testing your versatility. Listen carefully, be open to their suggestions, and give it your best shot!

8. Stay Positive: Keep a positive attitude, even if you're feeling nervous. Remember, everyone at the audition wants you to do well. Show them your passion and your determination. Even if you don't get the part, every audition is a step towards becoming a better actor.

9. Be Polite: And lastly, always be polite and respectful to everyone you meet. From the receptionist to the casting director, treat everyone kindly. Not only is it the right thing to do, but you never know who might be watching!

As we wrap up this treasure trove of tips, remember that auditioning is a journey, not a destination. You're going to learn something new from each audition, and you'll continue growing as an actor. Take these tips, be bold, and give it your best shot. And no matter what happens, know that you're already a superstar just for trying!

8 / getting an agent

agents of change: how an agent can propel your acting career

SO FAR, we've ventured into the worlds of acting techniques, auditions, and even handling the tough stuff like rejection. Now, we're going to explore another important part of an actor's journey: getting an agent. You might be wondering, what exactly does an agent do, and how can they help an actor's career? Well, buckle up, because we're about to dive into all of it.

Firstly, let's figure out what an agent is. In simplest terms, an acting agent is someone who helps actors find auditions and roles. They're like your own personal talent scout! They have lots of connections in the entertainment industry, and they use those connections to find opportunities that might be a good fit for you. They're also the ones who negotiate your contracts to make sure you're getting fair pay and treatment. Sounds like a pretty important job, right? It absolutely is!

Now, you may be thinking, "Why can't I just find auditions and negotiate contracts myself?" Well, you could, but it's a lot of work. And remember, your main job is to focus on your craft - on becoming the best actor you can be. An agent takes care of the business side of things so that you can devote your time and energy to your art.

Another cool thing about agents is that they can help you plan your career. They know a lot about the industry, and they can guide you towards roles that will help you grow as an actor. They can help you make decisions about which roles to take and which ones to pass on. It's like having a career coach who's there to help you navigate your path.

Now, not just any agent will do. You'll want to find an agent who really understands and believes in you. A good agent will know your strengths, see your potential, and be excited about your talent. They'll be your biggest cheerleader, always looking out for your best interests.

Getting an agent can seem like a big, scary step, but remember, an agent is there to help you. They work for you, not the other way around. You're the boss, and they're there to help you succeed.

It's also important to know that getting an agent doesn't guarantee success. It's just another tool in your actor's toolkit. It's still up to you to show up, give your best at every audition, and keep improving your skills.

So, how do you get an agent? The process can vary, but it often involves researching reputable agencies, sending them a headshot and resume, and sometimes performing a monologue or scene for them. It's a bit like auditioning for a role. We'll cover more about this process in a future chapter, so stay tuned!

As we bring this chapter to a close, remember that an agent is a partner in your acting journey. They can open doors for you and guide you along your path, but ultimately, you're the one in the driver's seat. And whether you have an agent or not, never forget that your talent, passion, and determination are the real stars of your acting career.

the agent adventure: when and how to consider getting an agent

We've been on quite a journey together, haven't we? Today, we're going to focus on a big question that might be dancing around in your heads - when and how should I consider getting an agent? We touched on what agents do in the previous chapter, but deciding when to embark on the agent adventure can be a bit tricky. Don't worry! We're going to untangle it together.

Now, you might be wondering why timing is important when considering getting an agent. Well, it's just like cooking. If you take the cookies out of the oven too soon, they're doughy. If you leave them in too long, they get burnt. Just like baking those perfect cookies, timing plays a crucial role in your acting career too.

Let's start with the "when." Knowing when to get an agent largely depends on you - your readiness, your level of experience, and your goals. It's usually beneficial to have some experience under your belt before you start looking for an agent. That's because agents are more likely to take you on if they see that you're dedicated, that you've been working on your craft, and that you have some roles (even small ones!) on your resume.

Getting an agent too soon can be like putting on a pair of shoes you're not ready to fill. You need to be ready for the opportunities an agent can provide. That means honing your acting skills, being comfortable auditioning, and understanding how to present yourself professionally. Acting classes, school plays, community theatre - these experiences help you build a solid foundation. You learn about acting techniques, how to work with others, and how to handle both praise and constructive criticism. All this prep work makes you agent-ready!

Now, let's move on to the "how." How do you go about getting an agent? This part can seem intimidating, but remember, every famous actor was once in your shoes. The first step is research. Look for reputable agencies that have good track records of representing young actors. Talk to your acting teachers, mentors, or any other actors you know. They can give you valuable insights and recommendations.

Once you've found some potential agents, the next step is reaching out to them. This usually involves sending them a package that includes your headshot, resume, and a cover letter. The cover letter should be a brief introduction about who you are, your acting experiences, and why you're interested in representation. It's like a friendly hello that gives them a peek into your acting journey.

Occasionally, you might be asked to audition for the agent. This could involve performing a monologue or a scene. Don't fret! This is just another opportunity to show off your acting skills. Remember, the agent wants to see you succeed. Your success is their success, too!

Getting an agent is a significant step in your acting journey. However, it's essential to remember that having an agent doesn't equate to instant success. It's a partnership where both sides have to work together. You still need to put in the hard work, attend auditions, keep learning, and stay passionate.

As we wrap up this chapter, keep in mind that your journey is uniquely yours. Some actors get agents early on, while others wait. There's no right or wrong timeline - only what feels right for you. So trust in your journey, keep honing your craft, and remember that every step, every role, and every experience is shaping you into the fantastic actor you're becoming.

conclusion: never stop dreaming

the actor's journey: embracing hard work, resilience, and patience

Isn't it exciting to imagine yourself in the spotlight, acting out fascinating stories and making people feel a whirlwind of emotions? Absolutely, it is! But you've probably figured out by now that the road to that dream is a journey—a fantastic, winding, challenging, and rewarding journey.

As we embark on this chapter, we're going to get real about the things that matter the most on your acting journey—hard work, resilience, and patience. They're like the magic ingredients that will flavor your journey, helping you become not just a good actor but an exceptional one!

Let's start with hard work. Acting isn't just about

Conclusion: Never Stop Dreaming

standing on a stage or in front of a camera and saying lines. It's about understanding the heart of a character, bringing them to life in a believable and touching way, and constantly improving your skills. This requires dedication and effort. Just like a musician practicing scales or a football player running drills, actors have to rehearse, study, and learn continuously.

Remember the story of the tortoise and the hare? The tortoise, though slow, wins the race because it keeps working consistently. Similarly, even if progress feels slow in your acting journey, consistent hard work will help you grow steadily and surely.

Now, let's talk about resilience. What's that, you ask? Well, resilience is like your superpower that helps you bounce back from difficulties or disappointments. In acting, you'll face moments where things won't go as planned. Perhaps you don't get a role you wanted, or someone gives you tough feedback. It's natural to feel upset during these times, but remember, these moments are not the end of your journey—they're just pit-stops along the way.

Think of every setback as a learning opportunity. Didn't land a role? Take a closer look at your audition. Was there something you could've done differently? Use these experiences as lessons to grow and improve. It's not about never falling—it's about always getting up and trying again. That's what resilience is all about!

Conclusion: Never Stop Dreaming

Finally, we have patience. In a world where we're used to getting things quickly, patience might seem like a tricky ingredient. However, in the acting world, things often take time. The role you dream of, the skills you want to master, the recognition you seek—all these things take time. But remember, great things often do!

Sometimes, it's about waiting for the right role that fits you perfectly. Other times, it's about giving yourself the time to learn and grow. Remember, a tree doesn't grow overnight. It takes time to grow from a tiny seed into a mighty oak. And just like that tree, your acting career will grow over time, too.

So, there you have it—hard work, resilience, and patience. These aren't just words; they're your companions on this fantastic journey. And you know what? They're going to make you stronger, wiser, and more prepared for the incredible adventures that await you.

Our next chapter will dive into something super fun: exploring different genres of acting. From drama to comedy, from horror to science fiction, every genre has its unique charm. So, get ready for another exciting journey into the wide world of acting.

Keep dreaming, keep growing, and remember: You're on an amazing journey,

learning, practicing, dreaming: your forever friends

Ready for our next adventure? That's terrific because we're diving into something that will light up your acting journey like a sparkler—always keeping learning, practicing, and dreaming. They're the heart of every actor's adventure, your constant companions that will accompany you as you traverse the thrilling road to acting stardom!

Let's start with learning, our first companion. Remember when we talked about the importance of education in acting? It's time to dig deeper into why learning never stops when you're an actor. Whether it's an acting technique, understanding a character, or exploring a new genre, every day brings a new opportunity to learn.

You may ask, "But why do I need to keep learning? Isn't knowing the basics enough?" That's a fantastic question! Think about this—imagine you're an explorer in a vast jungle. Sure, knowing how to read a map is essential, but isn't it exciting to discover new paths, unique plants, or hidden waterfalls? Similarly, in acting, the more you learn, the more you can bring to your performances, making them rich, diverse, and riveting.

Up next, we have practicing—our faithful

Conclusion: Never Stop Dreaming

companion that helps turn learning into action. Think about it—what's the use of learning how to ride a bicycle if you never actually try to ride one? That's where practicing comes in. It's your hands-on time with acting, where you take what you've learned and put it into action.

From rehearsing lines to working on your expressions in front of a mirror, every moment you spend practicing is a stepping stone to becoming a better actor. Remember, it's okay if you stumble or fumble while practicing—those moments are your best teachers! Practice helps you understand what works and what needs more work, making you more confident and skilled with each session.

Last but not least, let's talk about dreaming, our inspiring companion. If you think about it, every great journey starts with a dream, doesn't it? It was a dream that sparked your interest in acting and brought you this far into the exciting world of storytelling. Holding onto that dream and allowing it to grow is crucial.

Your dreams are your personal cheerleaders, reminding you why you fell in love with acting and giving you the strength to keep going, even when the journey feels tough. They keep your eyes on the prize —whether it's bringing a character to life, making an audience laugh, or receiving a standing ovation. Don't

Conclusion: Never Stop Dreaming

be afraid to dream big because dreams are where great adventures begin!

As we wrap up this chapter, remember that these three companions—learning, practicing, and dreaming—are here for the long haul. They're not just for beginners or professionals; they're for every actor, no matter where they are in their journey. Keep them close, nurture them, and watch as they illuminate your path in the magical world of acting.

Next up, we'll explore the exciting world of acting in different mediums. From stage to screen, and even animation voice-overs, we've got a thrilling journey ahead. So, buckle up, keep those companions close, and get ready for more acting adventures! Let's keep learning, practicing, and dreaming together, because that's what makes an actor's journey truly unforgettable.

Milton Keynes UK
Ingram Content Group UK Ltd.
UKHW021247191124
451300UK00008B/252